One-Hour
Holiday Crafts
for Kids

Cindy Groom Harry® and Staff, Designs & Consultation

HTS ❄ BOOKS
AN IMPRINT OF FOREST HOUSE™
School & Library Edition

Louis Weber, C.E.O.
Publications International, Ltd.
7373 North Cicero Avenue
Lincolnwood, Illinois 60646

8 7 6 5 4 3 2 1

ISBN: 0–7853–0961–6

Cindy Groom Harry is an author, crafts designer, and industry consultant whose work has been widely published in her own numerous craft books, and through hundreds of articles that have appeared in publications including *One-Hour Christmas Crafts For Kids, Better Homes and Gardens, McCall's Needlework and Crafts,* and *Craftworks for the Home.* She is a member of the Society of Craft Designers, where she previously served on the board of directors, and has also taught and demonstrated her designs on television craft programs.

Photography by
Sacco Productions Limited/Chicago

Photographer: Peter Ross

Photo Stylist: Paula Walters

Photo Shoot Production: Paula Walters

Illustrations by Cindy Groom Harry® and Staff, Designs & Consultation

Royal Model Management models: Sam Cikauskas, Shena Hollingsworth, Emeka Moka, Tara M. Rathsack

SOURCE OF MATERIALS

The following products were used in this book:
Aleene's™ Hot Stitch Fusible Web: 12; **Aleene's™ Shrink-It Plastic:** 19, 28; **Aleene's™ Tacky Glue:** 15, 25, 32, 42, 48, 54; **American Art Clay Co., Inc. Friendly Plastic®:** 6; **The Beadery® Beads:** 28, 45; **Black & Decker® 2 Temp™ Glue Gun and 2 Temp™ Glue Sticks:** 6, 9, 35, 38, 45, 48; **Crescent® Mat Board:** 45, 48; **Darice® Metallic Cord:** 38, 54; **DecoArt™ Americana™ Acrylic Spray Sealer:** 35; **Delta Ceramcoat™ Paint:** 22, 35; **Delta Glass Stain™:** 19; **Design Master® Color Tool Spray Paint:** 38; **Dow STYROFOAM®:** 48; **Duncan Scribbles® Dimensional Paint:** 6, 12, 19, 51, 54; **Fiskars® Scissors for Kids:** 9, 12, 15, 19, 22, 25, 28, 32, 35, 38, 42, 45, 48, 51, 54; **FloraCraft Blue Jay Chenille:** 42, 48; **Forster™ Head Beads:** 38; **Forster™ Doll Pin Stands:** 35, 38; **Forster™ Wood Beads:** 35; **Forster™ Woodsies:** 35; **Forster™ Dowels:** 38; **Hunt Bienfang® Foam Board:** 15; **Hunt Speedball® Painters® Paint Markers:** 25, 28, 32; **Hunt X-ACTO® Craft ¹⁄₁₆″ Burnisher:** 15; **Hunt X-ACTO® Craft Pointed Tweezers:** 45; **Hunt X-ACTO® Craft No. 1 Craft Knife:** 15; **Hygloss Super Glossy Poster Board:** 15; **Hygloss Paste on Wiggle Eyes:** 25, 35, 42, 48; **Hygloss Stick-A-Licks™:** 48; **Kunin/Foss Rainbow® Felt:** 9, 35, 42, 48, 54; **Kunin Varsity-Craft™ Pennant Felt:** 38, 54; **Magnetic Specialty, Inc. Magnetic Tape with Adhesive Backing:** 6, 42; **Magnetic Specialty, Inc. Craft MAGic Magnetic Sheeting with Adhesive:** 32; **The Punch Line™ All Purpose Craft Punches:** 25, 28; **Silver Brush, Ltd. Silverwhite™ Paint Brush:** 19, 22, 35; **Slomon's Stitchless™ Glue:** 12; **SPECIAL EDITION Select Fiberfill from Putnam Co. Inc:** 48; **V.I.P. Fabric:** 12; **Wang's International, Inc.® Felt Hat:** 48; **Wang's International, Inc.® Jingle Bells:** 42; **Wang's International, Inc.® Pearl Bead Garland:** 9; **Westrim® Crafts Fun Foam™:** 25; **Wrights® Lace:** 9; **Wrights® Rat Tail:** 9, 28, 42; **Wrights® Rick Rack:** 12, 54; **Wrights® Satin Ribbon:** 15, 25, 32, 45, 54.

contents

introduction

dear parents and teachers—

We know that most kids will be able to make the projects with little help, but there will be times when your assistance is needed. If the child has never used a glue gun, explain that both the nozzle and freshly applied glue are warm, even when the gun is set on low. Have a glass of water nearby just in case warm fingers need cooling. Occasionally, instructions direct the child to ask for adult help. Be sure everyone understands the "Important Things To Know" section on the facing page. The "General Pattern Instructions" section contains important instructions, too.

Most importantly, this should be an enjoyable, creative experience. Although we provide specific instructions, it's wonderful to see children create their own versions, using their own ideas. ENJOY!

hey kids—

Holidays can be extra special when you use your creativity! *One-Hour Holiday Crafts for Kids* shows you how to make a spooky Halloween game, pretty stained glass for Easter, a "fake" Valentine candy magnet, an adorable Thanksgiving turkey, and great projects for Christmas, Hanukkah, and Kwanzaa. You'll find cool crafts to work on all through the year!

One-Hour Holiday Crafts for Kids was made with you in mind. Many of the projects are fun things you can make by yourself. However, with some projects, you will need to ask an adult for help.

It's a good idea to make a project following the instructions exactly. Then feel free to make another, using your imagination, changing colors, adding a bit of yourself to make it even more yours. Think of all the variations you can make and all the gifts you can give!

Most important, HAVE FUN! Think how proud you'll be to say, "I made this myself!"

key:

Each project has been tested to measure the challenge level it presents to the crafter. The chart below shows you the key to the levels. Look for these stars above the title of each project.

easy   **medium**

challenging

general pattern instructions:

When the instructions for a project tell you to cut out a shape according to the pattern, begin by tracing the pattern from the book onto typing paper, using a pencil. If the pattern has an arrow with the word FOLD next to a line, it is a half pattern. Fold a sheet of typing paper in half and open up the paper. Place the fold line of the typing paper exactly on top of the fold line of the pattern and trace the pattern. Then refold and cut along the line, going through both layers of paper. Open paper for the full pattern.

To attach a pattern to fabric, roll 2-inch lengths of masking tape into circles with the adhesive side out. Attach the tape rolls to the back of the pattern in several places. Place pattern onto fabric and cut through both paper and fabric layers along the lines. If you are using a half pattern, open the pattern and tape the full pattern to the fabric. Cut on the edge of the pattern lines.

Even if you're anxious to get started, please read these few basic steps first:

1. Go through the book and decide what project you want to make first. Read the materials list and the instructions completely.

2. Gather all your materials, but remember to ask an adult for permission first! If you need to purchase materials, take along your book or make a shopping list so you know exactly what you need.

3. Prepare your work area ahead of time.

4. Be sure that an adult is nearby to offer help if you need it. Be sure to get help when you're working with an iron, glue gun, knife, or spray paint.

5. Do not put any materials near your mouth. Watch out for small items, like beads, around little kids and pets.

6. Use the glue gun on the low temperature setting, unless the directions tell you to put it on high. Do not touch the nozzle or freshly applied glue, because they may still be hot. Use the glue gun with adult permission only!

7. Wear an apron when painting with acrylic paints, because after the paint dries, it is permanent. If you do get it on your clothes, wash with soap and warm water immediately.

8. If you need to apply two coats of paint, let the first coat dry before painting the second.

9. When using spray paint or sealer, always work in a well-ventilated area. Shake the can well, put the object to be painted in a cardboard box, spray it with several light coats, and let it dry.

10. Clean up afterward, and put away all materials and tools.

Take a minute to look at the pictures below. the materials section for each project, you will find pictures of these frequently used items in addition to the other supplies needed. For example, if you see a picture of a glue bottle, that means you will need thick craft glue to complete that project.

pencil   ruler   children's scissors

water   glue gun   thick craft glue

paint brush   manicure scissors   tweezers

tape measure   straight pin   typing paper

washable fabric glue   iron   oven

masking tape   cardboard box   spatula

serrated knife   paper punch   fabric punch

valentine candy magnet

materials

- Moldable plastic: one red strip and one green strip, 1½ × 7 inches each

- One Valentine-print baking cup, 1½ inch diameter

- Brown or white dimensional squeeze paint
- 1-inch length of magnet strip, ½ inch wide

instructions

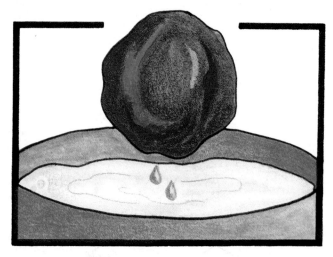

1 Place the strips of moldable plastic in warm water until they are softened. Knead and mix the two strips together until they are a uniform brown color. You may have to resoften the plastic a couple of times to remove all the streaks of red and green. Roll the plastic between your palms to form a smooth ball. Flatten one side of the ball slightly by gently pushing it down onto your work surface. Allow the plastic ball to set.

WITH LOVE

MOMMY

Glue the flattened side of the ball 2
into the bottom of the baking cup. Glue
the sides of the baking cup to the sides of
the ball in three or four places. Paint
wavy lines across the top of the ball with
the dimensional squeeze paint; let dry.

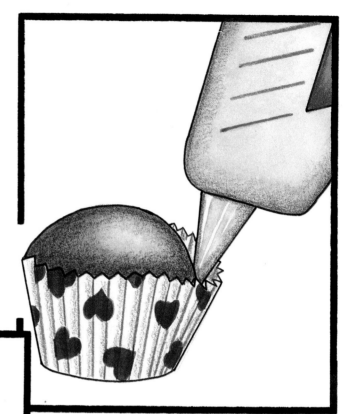

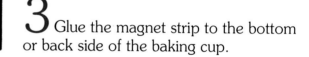

3 Glue the magnet strip to the bottom
or back side of the baking cup.

sweetheart sachet

materials

- 5 × 5-inch square of mauve felt
- 5 × 5-inch square of white flat lace
- Potpourri

- 13-inch length of white gathered lace, ½ inch wide
- 12-inch length of 4mm string pearls

- 2-inch length of white rattail cord
- Gold charm

instructions

1 Using the pattern on page 58, trace and cut one felt heart and one flat lace heart. Glue the two hearts together along the edges, leaving the bottom point of the heart unglued. Gently stuff the heart with potpourri, and then glue the point closed.

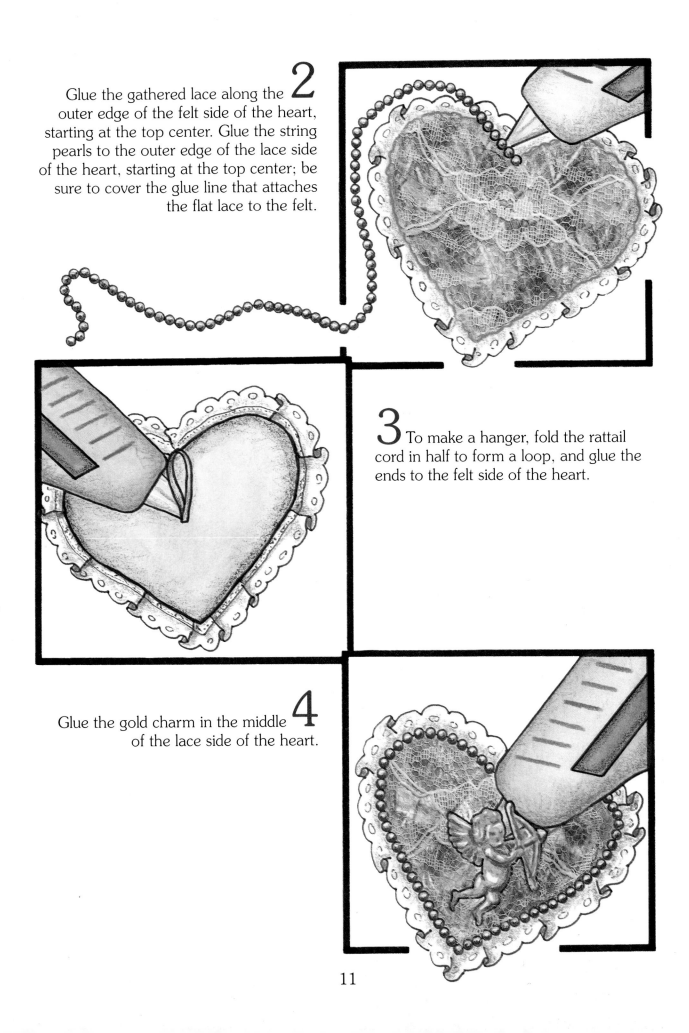

2 Glue the gathered lace along the outer edge of the felt side of the heart, starting at the top center. Glue the string pearls to the outer edge of the lace side of the heart, starting at the top center; be sure to cover the glue line that attaches the flat lace to the felt.

3 To make a hanger, fold the rattail cord in half to form a loop, and glue the ends to the felt side of the heart.

4 Glue the gold charm in the middle of the lace side of the heart.

easter egg sweatshirt

materials

- Fabric: 8 × 10 inches multicolored print; 4 × 10 inches coordinating purple small print; 4 × 5 inches coordinating pink small print; 4 × 5 inches coordinating green small print

- 10 × 16-inch piece of fusible webbing
- Turquoise sweatshirt

- 2-yard length of jumbo multicolored rickrack
- Pink dimensional squeeze paint

instructions

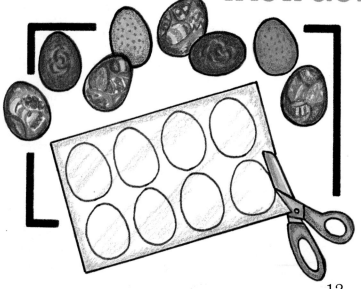

1 Using the pattern on page 58, trace and cut four eggs from the multicolored fabric, two eggs from the purple fabric, one egg from the pink fabric, and one egg from the green fabric. Using the same pattern, trace and cut eight eggs from the fusible webbing.

Lay the fabric eggs on the front of 2 the sweatshirt in different patterns until you find an arrangement you like. Use the fusible webbing to adhere the fabric eggs to the front of the shirt according to the manufacturer's instructions.

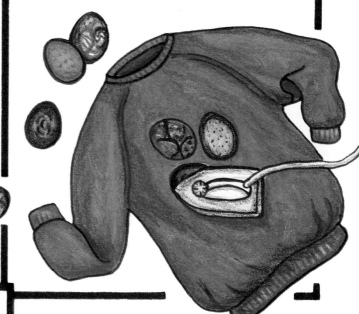

3 Cut seven 3-inch lengths of rickrack. Arrange two lengths of rickrack on each of the pink and green eggs, and three lengths of rickrack on one of the purple eggs. Trim the rickrack ends even with the edges of the eggs, and then glue the rickrack on the eggs with washable fabric glue. Measure the neckline and cuffs of the shirt, and then measure and cut corresponding lengths of rickrack. Glue the rickrack to the neckline and cuffs of the shirt with fabric glue so that the ends meet at the seams of the shirt.

Paint around each egg with the 4 dimensional squeeze paint to cover the edges of the fabric; let dry.

button quilt

materials

- 7½ × 7½-inch piece of foam board, ½ inch thick
- Fabric: 6 × 6 inches coordinating blue print; 6 × 6 inches coordinating pink print; 6 × 11 inches coordinating green print

- 4-inch length of coordinating satin ribbon, ⅛ inch wide

- 7¼ × 7¼-inch piece of white posterboard
- Nine coordinating buttons, ½ inch diameter

instructions

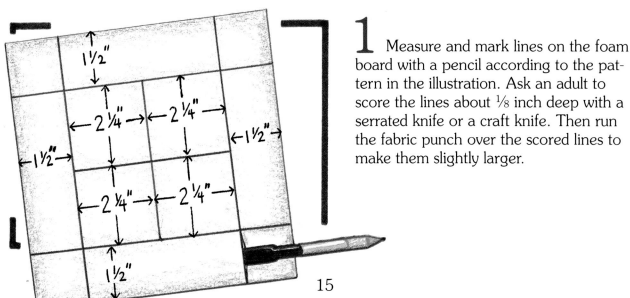

1½"
2¼" 2¼"
1½" 1½"
2¼" 2¼"
1½"

1 Measure and mark lines on the foam board with a pencil according to the pattern in the illustration. Ask an adult to score the lines about ⅛ inch deep with a serrated knife or a craft knife. Then run the fabric punch over the scored lines to make them slightly larger.

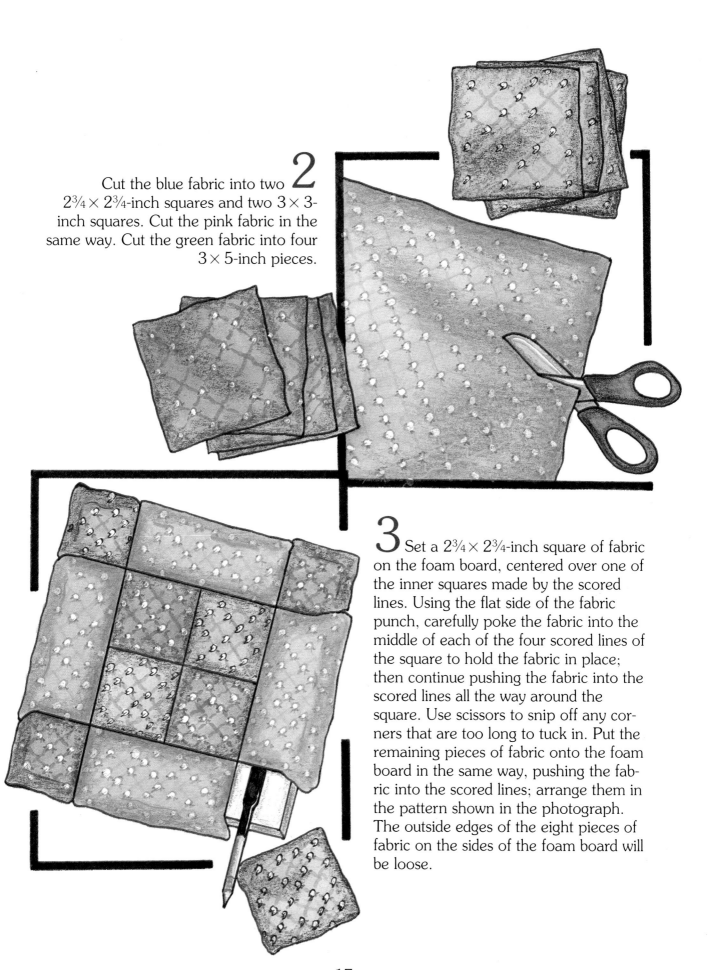

2 Cut the blue fabric into two $2\frac{3}{4} \times 2\frac{3}{4}$-inch squares and two 3×3-inch squares. Cut the pink fabric in the same way. Cut the green fabric into four 3×5-inch pieces.

3 Set a $2\frac{3}{4} \times 2\frac{3}{4}$-inch square of fabric on the foam board, centered over one of the inner squares made by the scored lines. Using the flat side of the fabric punch, carefully poke the fabric into the middle of each of the four scored lines of the square to hold the fabric in place; then continue pushing the fabric into the scored lines all the way around the square. Use scissors to snip off any corners that are too long to tuck in. Put the remaining pieces of fabric onto the foam board in the same way, pushing the fabric into the scored lines; arrange them in the pattern shown in the photograph. The outside edges of the eight pieces of fabric on the sides of the foam board will be loose.

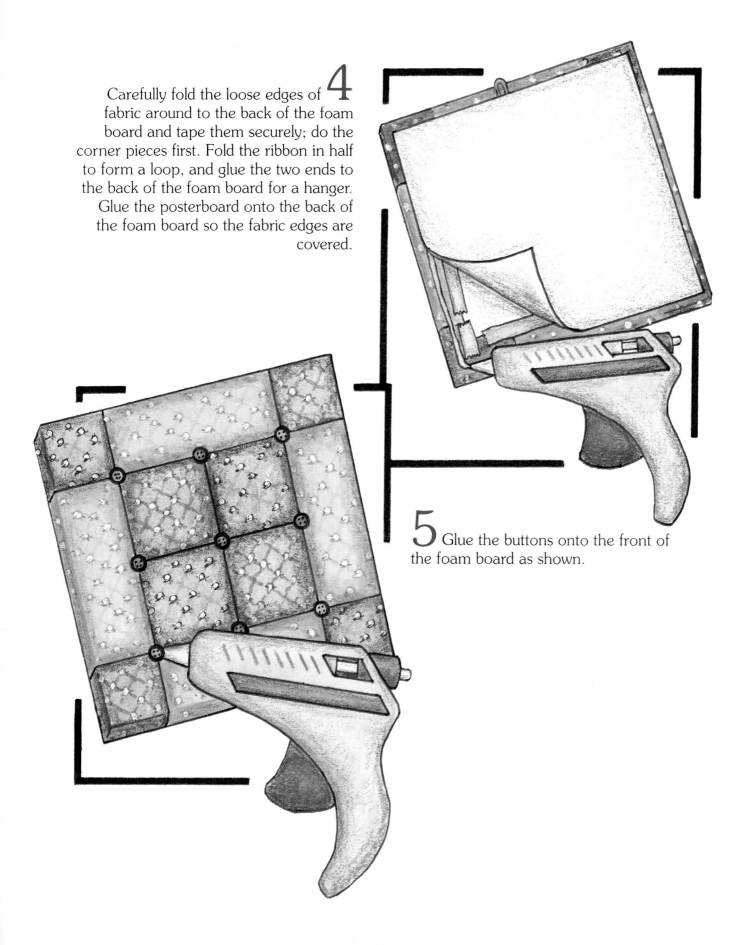

Carefully fold the loose edges of **4**
fabric around to the back of the foam
board and tape them securely; do the
corner pieces first. Fold the ribbon in half
to form a loop, and glue the two ends to
the back of the foam board for a hanger.
Glue the posterboard onto the back of
the foam board so the fabric edges are
covered.

5 Glue the buttons onto the front of
the foam board as shown.

stained glass easter basket

- 5 × 7-inch piece of clear shrink plastic
- 8 × 10-inch piece of cardboard

- Black dimensional squeeze paint

- Glass stain: red, green, blue, yellow, purple, orange

instructions

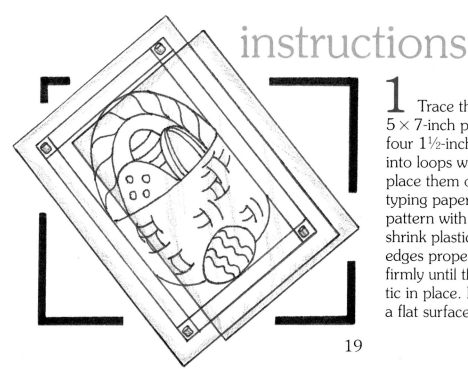

1 Trace the pattern on page 59 onto a 5 × 7-inch piece of typing paper. Roll four 1½-inch lengths of masking tape into loops with the sticky side out, and place them on the four corners of the typing paper; do not cover any of the pattern with the tape. Set the piece of shrink plastic on the pattern with the edges properly aligned and press down firmly until the tape holds the shrink plastic in place. Place it on the cardboard on a flat surface

19

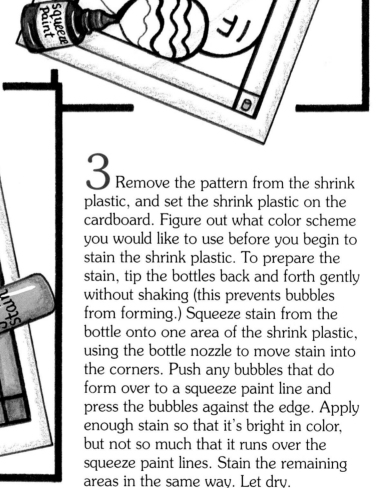

Beginning with the horizontal line 2 at the top of the pattern and working your way down, carefully trace the pattern onto the shrink plastic with the squeeze paint. It is important that all the lines and corners are solid so the different areas of the pattern are separated. If the paint smears, use a damp paint brush to wipe away the smear. Let dry.

3 Remove the pattern from the shrink plastic, and set the shrink plastic on the cardboard. Figure out what color scheme you would like to use before you begin to stain the shrink plastic. To prepare the stain, tip the bottles back and forth gently without shaking (this prevents bubbles from forming.) Squeeze stain from the bottle onto one area of the shrink plastic, using the bottle nozzle to move stain into the corners. Push any bubbles that do form over to a squeeze paint line and press the bubbles against the edge. Apply enough stain so that it's bright in color, but not so much that it runs over the squeeze paint lines. Stain the remaining areas in the same way. Let dry.

patriotic t-shirt

materials

- White T-shirt
- T-shirt board or 18 × 21-inch piece of stiff cardboard covered with plastic wrap

- Acrylic paint: red, blue
- Two plastic lids, 4–5 inches in diameter

- Sponges: 4-inch star (or cut star shape from 4-inch square sponge using pattern on page 58); 2 × 3-inch rectangle

instructions

1 Launder the shirt before you begin so that the paint will adhere better; do not use a fabric softener. Dry and press the shirt with an iron if necessary. Stretch the shirt onto the shirt board. (This prevents paint from soaking through to the back of the shirt.)

22

2 Pour some blue paint onto one plastic lid. Use a paintbrush to spread the paint into a circle about 4 inches across. Press the star sponge into the paint until the sponge surface is covered with paint, but not saturated; then press the star sponge onto typing paper to practice stamping. Some white should show through the paint for a "sponged" look. Dip the star sponge in the paint before you make each stamp. When you're ready, randomly paint about ten stars on the shirt. Let the stars dry.

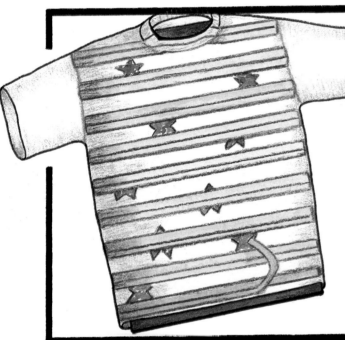

3 Attach a length of masking tape horizontally across the front of the shirt at the top. Overlap three or four more lengths of tape onto the first one until you have a stripe of tape 1¾ inches wide on the shirt. Put a light pencil mark on the shirt 1¾ inches from the bottom of the tape. Repeat the taping procedure below that mark. Continue measuring and making 1¾-inch stripes of tape this way, leaving 1¾-inch stripes of uncovered shirt between them, until you get to the bottom of the shirt.

4 Prepare the red paint in the other plastic lid as you did with the blue paint. Practice painting with the rectangular sponge until you can do it neatly. Then begin stamping the uncovered bands of shirt between the bands of tape. Paint as close as you can to the blue stars, but be careful not to get any red paint on them. Continue stamping until all the bands of shirt are painted red. Let the paint dry, and then remove the masking tape from the shirt. You can wear the shirt right away, but do not wash it for 48 hours.

halloween
mobile

materials

- Foam sheet: 5 × 5 inches yellow; 3 × 6 inches orange; 3 × 7 inches white; 5 × 5 inches black

- Fine-point opaque paint markers: black, brown
- Wiggle eyes: eighteen 12mm; four 5mm

- 58-inch length of black satin ribbon, ⅛-inch wide
- ¼-inch black pom

instructions

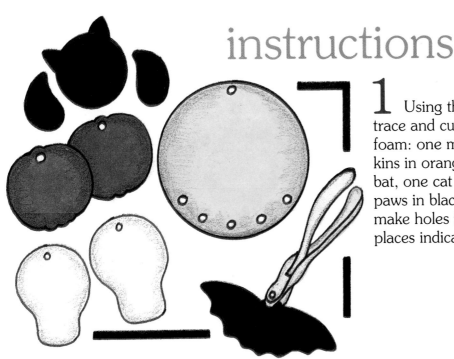

1 Using the patterns on page 60, trace and cut the following shapes from foam: one moon in yellow; two pumpkins in orange; two skulls in white; one bat, one cat head, and one set of cat paws in black. Use the paper punch to make holes in the foam shapes in the places indicated on the patterns.

2 Decorate both sides of the pumpkins by drawing lines with the brown marker and faces with the black marker; let dry. Draw faces on both sides of the skulls with the black marker; let dry. Glue two 5mm eyes on both sides of the bat. Glue two 12mm eyes on both sides of the pumpkins and skulls.

3 Cut a 12-inch length of ribbon. Insert one end of the ribbon 1½ inches into the single hole at the top of the moon. Tie a double knot in the ribbon to securely attach it to the moon. Trim the short end of the ribbon close to the knot. Position and glue the cat head on the back upper side of the moon. Position and glue the cat paws on the front of the moon, with the right paw covering the ribbon hanger. Glue the black pom nose on the cat head so that it slightly overlaps the edge of the moon, and glue two 12mm eyes to the cat head.

4 Cut the remaining ribbon into the following lengths, and use double knots to tie one end of each length to a foam shape and the other end to a hole at the bottom of the moon: a 6-inch length for one pumpkin; a 9-inch length for one skull; a 13-inch length for the bat; an 11-inch length for one pumpkin; a 7-inch length for one skull. Trim the ends of each length of ribbon close to the knots.

witch's necklace

materials

- 8¼ × 10¾-inch piece of opaque shrink plastic
- Medium-point opaque paint markers: black, orange, purple, green

- 30-inch length of black rattail cord

- Beads: 20 orange pony beads, 6 × 9mm each; six black melon pony beads, 10mm each

instructions

1 Using the patterns on page 61, trace the ghost, bat, and witch shapes onto the shrink plastic with the black paint marker. You may want to tape the shrink plastic on top of the patterns to hold it in place.

Trace the faces and other details **2** from the patterns onto the shapes with the paint markers using the colors shown in the drawing. Use a smooth back-and-forth motion when you color so you cover the shrink plastic evenly. Let each color dry completely before adding the next color. Opaque plastic will appear white when it shrinks, so you don't have to color any areas that should be white.

When the paint is dry, cut out each shape along its outline. Use the paper punch to make two holes in each shape in the places indicated on the patterns.

3 Get help from an adult for this step. Bake the shapes in the oven according to the manufacturer's directions. (Note: Do not remove the shapes from the oven until they have completely flattened. Use a spatula to separate them if parts stick to each other while baking and to press them after you take them from the oven.) When the shapes are done baking, remove them from the oven and let them cool.

Insert one end of the rattail cord 4
through the holes on the witch's hat and
slide the witch to the middle of the cord.
(Hold the two ends of the cord together
in one hand and pull on the witch with
the other hand to make sure it is in the
middle, and keep it in the middle as you
work.) Slide two orange beads, one black
bead, and two more orange beads onto
the cord on the right side of the witch.
Slide the ghost onto the cord on the right
side of the beads, and then slide two
orange beads, one black bead, two
orange beads, one black bead, and two
orange beads onto the cord on the right
side of the ghost. Tie a knot in the cord
to the right of the last bead.

5 Slide two orange beads, one black
bead, and two orange beads onto the
cord on the left side of the witch. Slide
the bat onto the cord on the left side of
the beads, and then slide two orange
beads, one black bead, two orange
beads, one black bead, and two orange
beads onto the cord on the left side of
the bat. Tie a knot in the cord to the left
of the last bead. Tie together the ends of
the cord to finish the necklace.

spooky
tic-tac-toe

materials

- Magnetic sheeting: one black 5 × 5-inch piece; one orange and one white 1½ × 7½-inch piece

- Fine-point opaque paint markers: black, brown

- 20-inch length of green satin ribbon, ⅛ inch wide

instructions

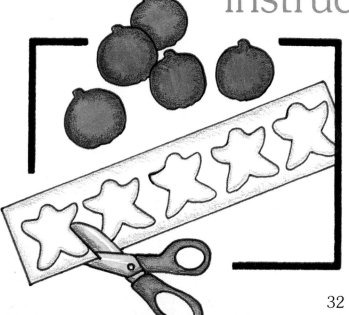

1 Using the patterns on page 59, trace and cut five pumpkins from the orange magnetic sheeting and five ghosts from the white magnetic sheeting. When cutting the magnetic sheeting, use regular scissors most of the time, and use small manicure scissors for small curves.

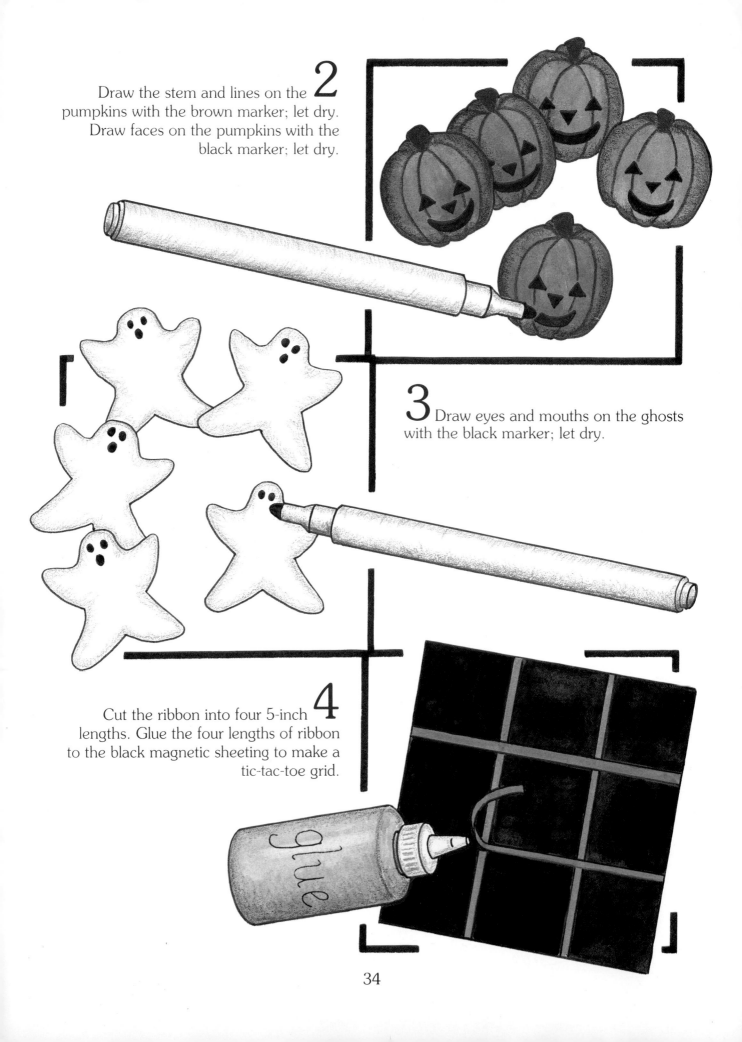

Draw the stem and lines on the 2
pumpkins with the brown marker; let dry.
Draw faces on the pumpkins with the
black marker; let dry.

3 Draw eyes and mouths on the ghosts
with the black marker; let dry.

Cut the ribbon into four 5-inch 4
lengths. Glue the four lengths of ribbon
to the black magnetic sheeting to make a
tic-tac-toe grid.

glue

turkey table favor

materials

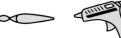

- Acrylic paint: brown, yellow, red, orange
- 1⅛-inch wooden doll pin base
- Wooden balls: 1¾-inch diameter; 1¼-inch diameter

- Pre-cut teardrop wood pieces: eleven 2-inch (size D); two 1½-inch (size E)
- Acrylic spray sealer

- Felt: 1 × 2 inches orange; 1 × 2 inches red
- Two wiggle eyes, 8mm each

instructions

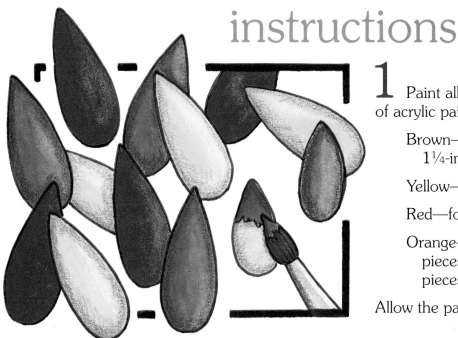

1 Paint all wood pieces with two coats of acrylic paint in the following colors:

Brown—doll pin base, 1¾-inch ball, 1¼-inch ball

Yellow—four 2-inch teardrop pieces

Red—four 2-inch teardrop pieces

Orange—three 2-inch teardrop pieces; two 1½-inch teardrop pieces.

Allow the paint to dry between coats.

To make the body, glue the **2**
1¾-inch wooden ball to the doll pin
base. To make the head, glue the
1¼-inch wooden ball to the
front top of the body.

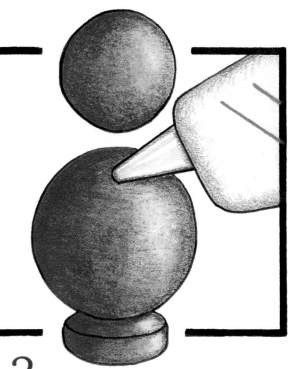

3 To make the feathers, arrange the
large teardrop pieces in the color order
shown in the illustration. Overlap the
edges of the teardrop pieces and glue
them together so they form a half-circle
of feathers. Glue the half-circle of feathers to the body at the center and at each
end of the half-circle. To make the wings,
glue one small teardrop piece to each
side of the body. Lightly spray the turkey
with acrylic sealer using the spray-painting technique described in the Introduction; let dry.

To make the beak, use the pattern **4**
on page 59 to trace and cut two
triangles from the orange felt; align the
two short sides of each triangle and glue
them to the center front of the head.
To make the wattle, use the pattern on
page 59 to trace and cut the wattle from
the red felt; glue the top of the wattle to
the head just below the beak.
Glue the wiggle eyes to the head above
the beak.

hanukkah banner

materials

- Pennant felt: 17 × 20 inches navy blue; 11 × 13 inches gold; 3½ × 7 inches white
- Gold spray paint

- 18-inch wooden dowel, ½ inch diameter
- Two 1⅛-inch wooden doll pin bases
- Two 1¼-inch wooden head beads

- 19-inch length of gold fringe, 4 inches wide
- 28-inch length of gold metallic cord

instructions

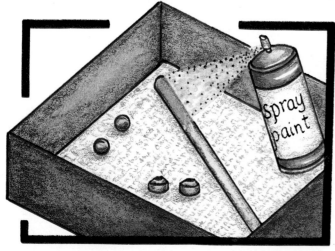

1 Using the pattern on page 62, trace and cut the menorah from the gold felt. Working with an adult in a well-ventilated area, spray the menorah with two coats of gold spray paint; let dry. Spray the dowel, the two doll pin bases, and the two head beads with two coats of gold spray paint; let dry. Use the spray-painting technique described in the Introduction.

To make a hem in the 17-inch side 2 of the blue felt, fold over 2 inches of the felt and crease it. Unfold, apply a line of glue ¼ inch from the edge, and refold the felt. Hold it in place until the glue dries. Be sure to leave enough room between the crease and the glue line to insert the dowel.

3 Using the patterns on page 62, trace and cut nine candles from the white pennant felt and nine flames from the gold pennant felt.

Glue the fringe to the bottom of the **4**
banner so that 1 inch of fringe sticks out
from each side. Fold and glue the 1-inch
sections of fringe to the back of the banner. Position the menorah and candles as
in the illustration, and then glue them to
the banner. Roll nine 1½-inch lengths of
masking tape into loops with the sticky
side out, and put one on the back of each
flame. (You can add one flame to the
banner on each day of Hanukkah.)

5 Slide the dowel through the hem at
the top of the banner. Glue a head bead
to a doll pin base, and then glue them to
one end of the dowel. Repeat on the
other end of the dowel. To make a hanger, tie the ends of the cord to the ends of
the dowel.

pom reindeer magnet

materials

- Poms: 1-inch beige; 2-inch brown; ¼-inch red
- Felt: 1 × 1 inches red; 2 × 2 inches brown
- Two wiggle eyes, 10mm each

- Two beige chenille stems, 12 inches each
- 12-inch length of red rattail cord

- Two gold jingle bells, 8mm each
- ¾-inch length of magnet strip, ½ inch wide

instructions

1 To make the head and the muzzle, glue the beige pom to the lower front part of the brown pom. For the nose, glue the red pom to the upper front part of the muzzle. Cut a smiling mouth shape from the red felt, and glue it below the nose. Glue the wiggle eyes to the head so that the bottom edges of the eyes touch the top of the muzzle.

DEaR SaNXA,
i hopE YoU
Like Your
miLK and
Cookies.
LoVE,
Jamie

Measure and cut one chenille stem **2**
into a 5-inch length and a 7-inch length.
Measure and cut the other chenille stem
into two 6-inch lengths; you will use only
one of the 6-inch lengths, so set the
other one aside. To make the antlers, line
up the middles of the three lengths of
chenille stem. Twist the stems in the middle to join them together. Arrange the
stems so the 7-inch length is on the bottom, the 6-inch length is in between, and
the 5-inch length is on top. Pinch and
curl each of the six ends up to form the
antlers, as in the drawing. Glue the middle of the antlers to the back of the head.

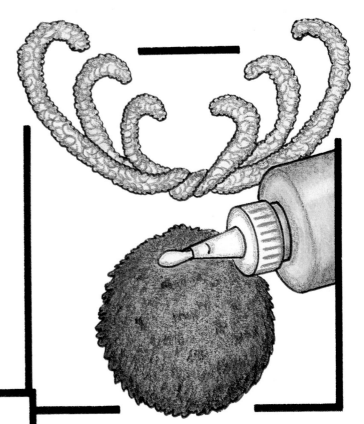

3 Using the pattern on page 62, trace
and cut two ears from the brown felt.
Apply a dot of glue to the bottom of one
ear; pinch the bottom together and hold
it for a moment. Repeat this gluing
process to make the other ear. Glue the
ears to the head just in front of the
antlers.

Tie a bow in the rattail cord. Tie a **4**
jingle bell to each end of the rattail cord.
Glue the bow beneath the muzzle. Glue
the magnet strip to the back of the head.

pine cone wreath

materials

- 5 × 5-inch square of brown mat board or cardboard
- Pine cones: about fifteen 1 inch in diameter; about thirty ½ inch in diameter

- 8mm round beads: seven red; eight green
- 15-inch length of red and green plaid ribbon, ⅝ inch wide

- 8-inch length of red satin ribbon, ⅛ inch wide

instructions

1 Using the pattern on page 63, trace and cut a circle from the mat board. Glue the 1-inch pine cones standing upright in a circle on the mat board; arrange them so they fit tightly against each other.

2 Glue about half of the ½-inch pine cones on their sides on the outer edge of the mat board in the spaces between the 1-inch pine cones. Glue the rest of the ½-inch pine cones around the inner edge of the mat board in the same way. It might be easier for you to arrange the pine cones if you use tweezers.

3 Glue the beads onto the wreath as shown in the illustration.

4 Tie a bow in the plaid ribbon, and cut "V" notches in the tail ends. Glue the bow to the top of the wreath. To make a hanger, fold the satin ribbon in half to form a loop, and glue the ends to the back of the mat board at the top of the wreath.

christmas
cowboy

materials

- 7 × 7-inch piece of white cardboard
- White foam balls: one 3½-inch diameter; one 2½-inch diameter; six 1-inch diameter
- White fiberfill
- Felt: 7 × 7-inch piece red; 1 × 1-inch piece orange

- 1-inch wide yellow star sticker
- Two wiggle eyes, 12mm each
- 6¼-inch length of red chenille stem
- Two green poms, 1-inch each
- 4-inch brown felt cowboy hat

- Small holly sprig
- 1-inch wreath
- Two small wrapped gifts
- Two ornaments, ½-inch each

instructions

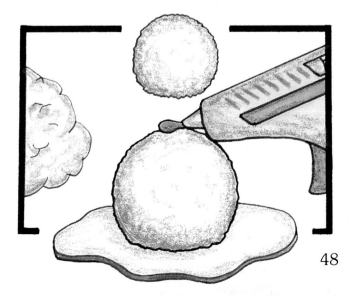

1 For the base, trim the edges of the cardboard into an irregular curved shape. Slightly flatten one side of the large foam ball by pushing it firmly against the work surface. Glue the flat side of the ball to the center of the cardboard base. Slightly flatten one side of the small foam ball, and then glue the flat side to the top of the large ball. Fluff up the fiberfill, and glue it to the cardboard base.

Using the pattern on page 58, trace **2**
and cut the vest from the red felt. Cut
¾-inch slits around the bottom of the
vest to create the fringe. Wrap the vest
around the body of the snowman and
glue it in place. Attach the star sticker to
the vest. To make the arm, glue three
1-inch foam balls to the side of the snowman, starting at the vest's arm hole and
moving down to the tummy. Repeat on
the other side for the other arm.

3 Glue the wiggle eyes on the snowman's face. Using the pattern on page
58, trace and cut the nose from orange
felt, and then glue it to the face. Cut a
1¼-inch piece of the chenille stem, bend
it into a smile, and then glue it to the
face. Bend a ½-inch section at each end
of the remaining 5-inch length of chenille
stem. Insert one ½-inch end into the side
of the snowman's head, curve the stem
across the top of the head, and insert the
other ½-inch end into the other side of
the head. Glue the green poms over the
ends of the stems.

Glue the hat to the top of the snow- **4**
man's head. Glue the sprig of holly to the
hatband. Glue the wreath in front of the
snowman's hand, and glue the gifts and
ornaments in the snow.

christmas window decorations

materials

- Five 6 × 6-inch pieces of cardboard
- Dimensional squeeze paint: red, white, green, glittering gold
- Plastic wrap

instructions

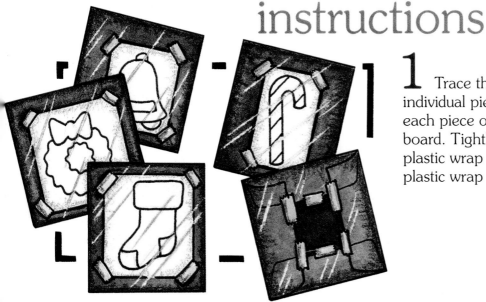

1 Trace the patterns on page 64 onto individual pieces of paper, and then tape each piece of paper to a piece of cardboard. Tightly cover each pattern with plastic wrap and tape the edges of the plastic wrap to the back of the cardboard.

51

Carefully paint the plastic wrap **2** using the pattern as a guide; refer to the photograph for color direction. Work with one color at a time and let each color set for ten minutes before you paint with the next color. To begin painting, outline the part of the pattern you're going to paint; lightly touch the tip of the bottle to the plastic wrap, carefully squeeze the bottle, and pull (don't push) the tip along the outline; the paint should be about ⅛ inch thick. Then paint inside the outlined area, working from left to right and top to bottom. If you make a mistake, wipe the paint off with a paper towel. If the tip of the bottle clogs, use a straight pin to open the hole and then squeeze a bit of paint on a paper scrap to regain a smooth flow.

3 Let the paint dry for 24 hours. Then peel the decorations off the plastic wrap. Trim off any paint that has spread beyond the outline of the decoration.

kwanzaa
calendar

materials

- Felt: 8 × 11 inches red;
  8 × 11 inches green;
  8 × 8 inches yellow
- Glittering gold dimensional squeeze paint

- 2-yard 4-inch length of yellow satin ribbon, 1 inch wide
- 16 × 20-inch piece of black pennant felt

- 4-yard 8-inch length of medium-width bright green rickrack
- 1-yard 14-inch length of gold metallic cord

instructions

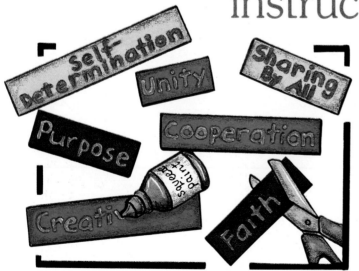

1 Cut three green, two yellow, and two red 1 × 5-inch pieces of felt. Carefully write the following words on the felt using squeeze paint (you may want to practice writing the words first on scrap paper): *Unity, Self-Determination, Purpose, Creativity, Sharing By All, Cooperation,* and *Faith*. Let the paint dry, and then trim the ends of the felt pieces to within ¼ inch of the words.

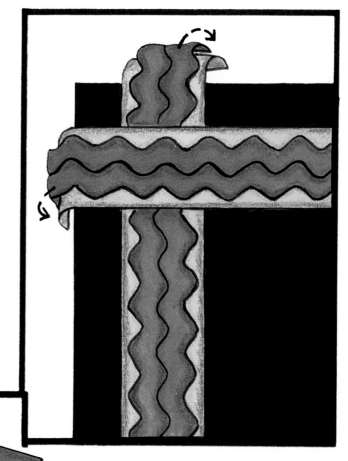

2 Cut the ribbon into two 17-inch lengths and two 21-inch lengths. Cut the rickrack into four 17-inch lengths and four 21-inch lengths. Glue the 17-inch lengths of ribbon vertically on the black felt, ½ inch from the sides. Glue two 17-inch lengths of rickrack side by side on top of each 17-inch length of ribbon. Fold and glue the ends of the 17-inch pieces of ribbon and rickrack over to the back of the black felt. Glue the 21-inch lengths of ribbon horizontally on the black felt, ½ inch from the sides. Glue two 21-inch lengths of rickrack side by side on top of each 21-inch length of ribbon. Fold and glue the ends of the 21-inch pieces of ribbon and rickrack over to the back of the black felt.

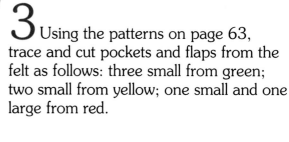

3 Using the patterns on page 63, trace and cut pockets and flaps from the felt as follows: three small from green; two small from yellow; one small and one large from red.

Arrange the pockets, flaps, and **4** words on the black felt as shown in the illustration. To glue the pockets to the black felt, glue the bottom of each pocket first, and then slightly push in the sides of the pocket and glue them. (This will loosen the pockets to allow space for gifts.) Glue the top edge of the flaps about ¼ inch above the pockets. Glue the words above the flaps.

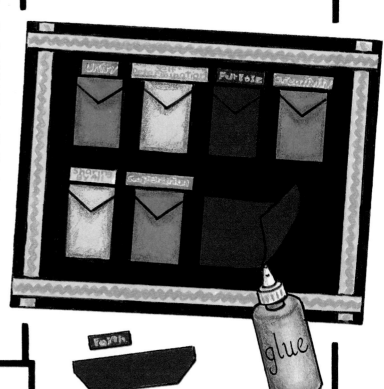

5 Cut seven 6-inch lengths of gold cord. Tie a bow in each length, and then evenly trim the ends. Glue one bow to each pocket flap. Turn the calendar over. For hanger loops, cut two 4-inch lengths of gold cord. Fold each length in half to form a loop, and glue the ends of one loop in each of the top corners on the back of the calendar.

patterns

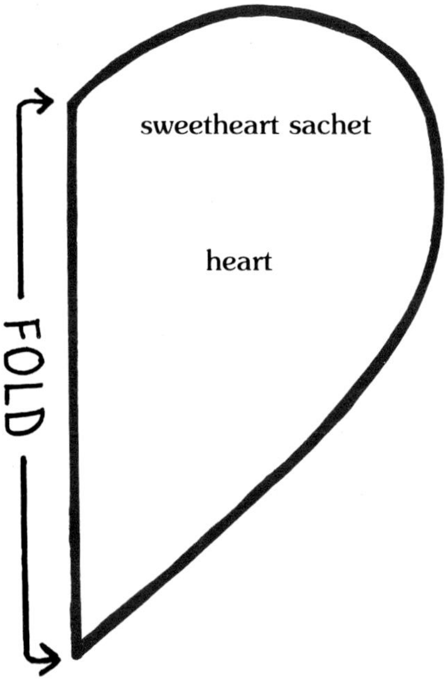

sweetheart sachet

heart

FOLD

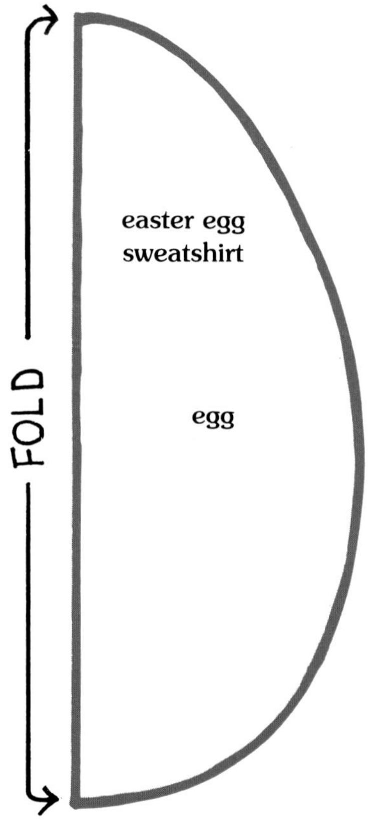

easter egg
sweatshirt

egg

FOLD

christmas cowboy

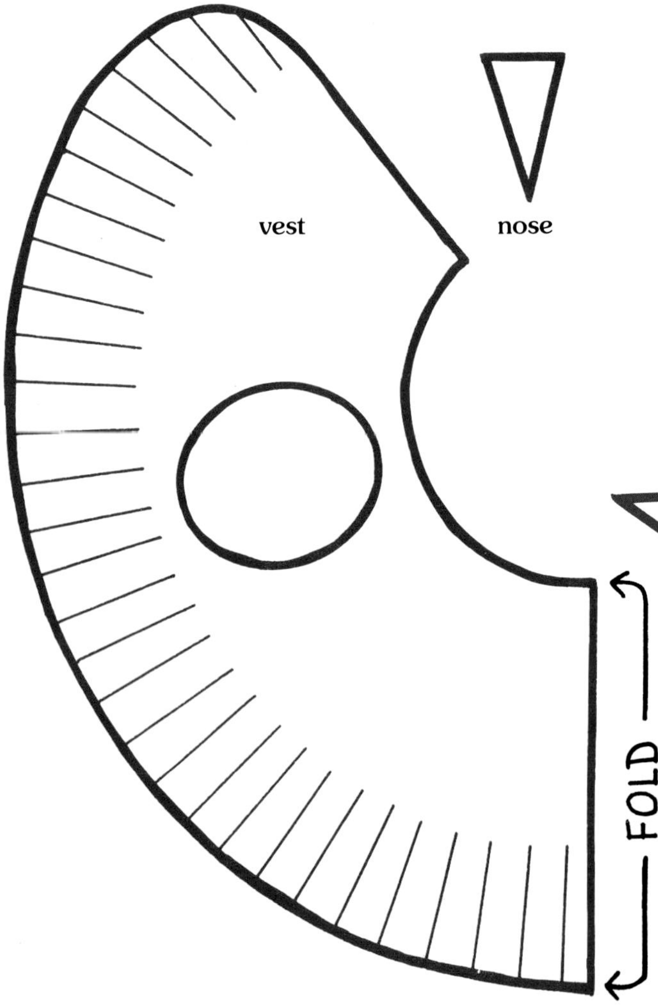

vest

nose

patriotic t-shirt

star

FOLD

58

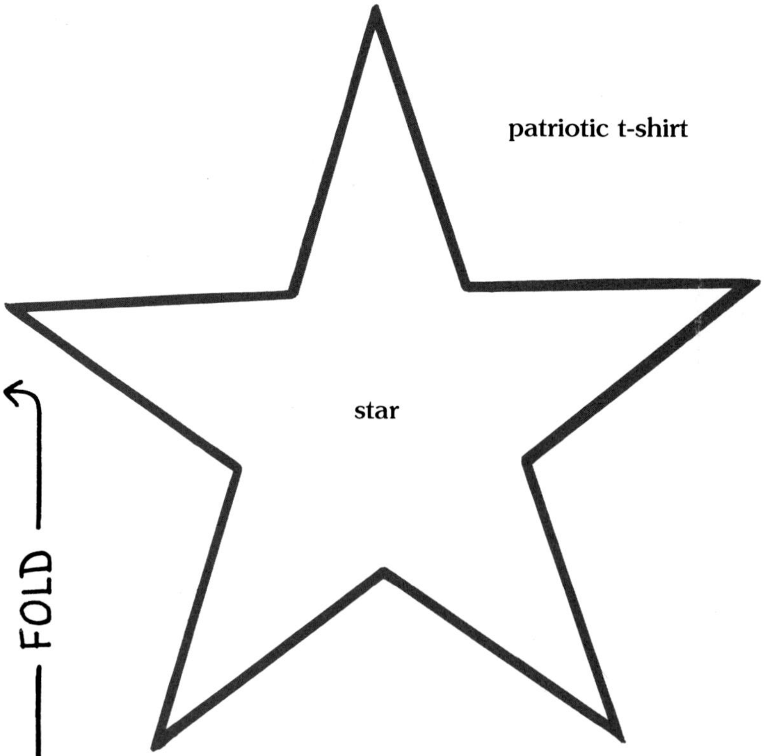

stained glass easter basket

spooky tic-tac-toe

pumpkin (cut 5)

ghost
(cut 5)

turkey table favor

beak

(cut 2)

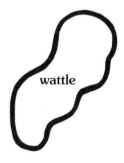

wattle

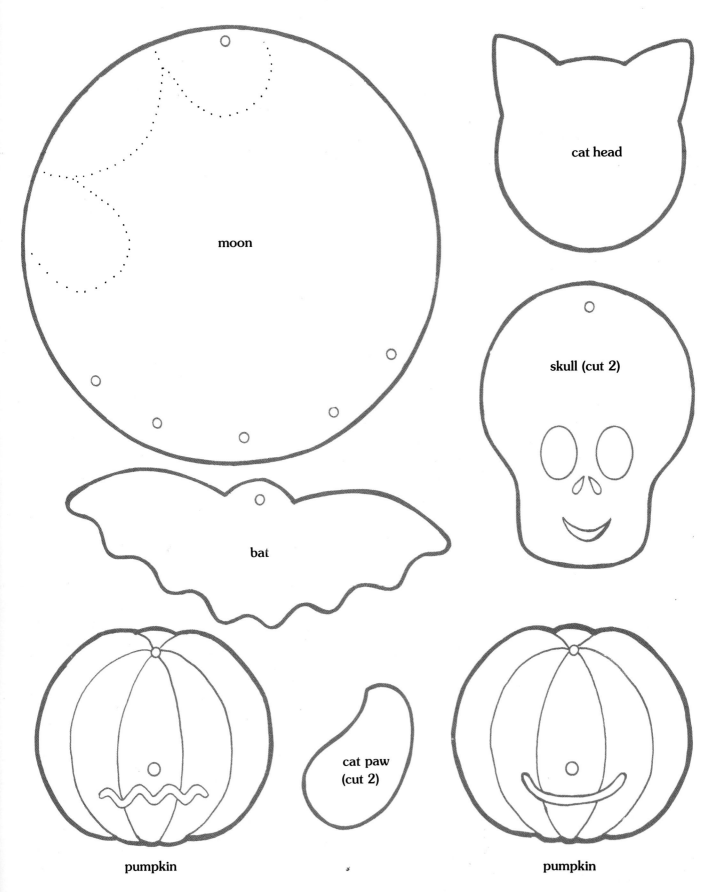

moon

cat head

skull (cut 2)

bat

pumpkin

cat paw
(cut 2)

pumpkin

witch's necklace

bat

ghost

witch

hanukkah banner

pom reindeer magnet

ear
(cut 2)

FOLD

menorah

candle (cut 9)

flame
(cut 9)

62

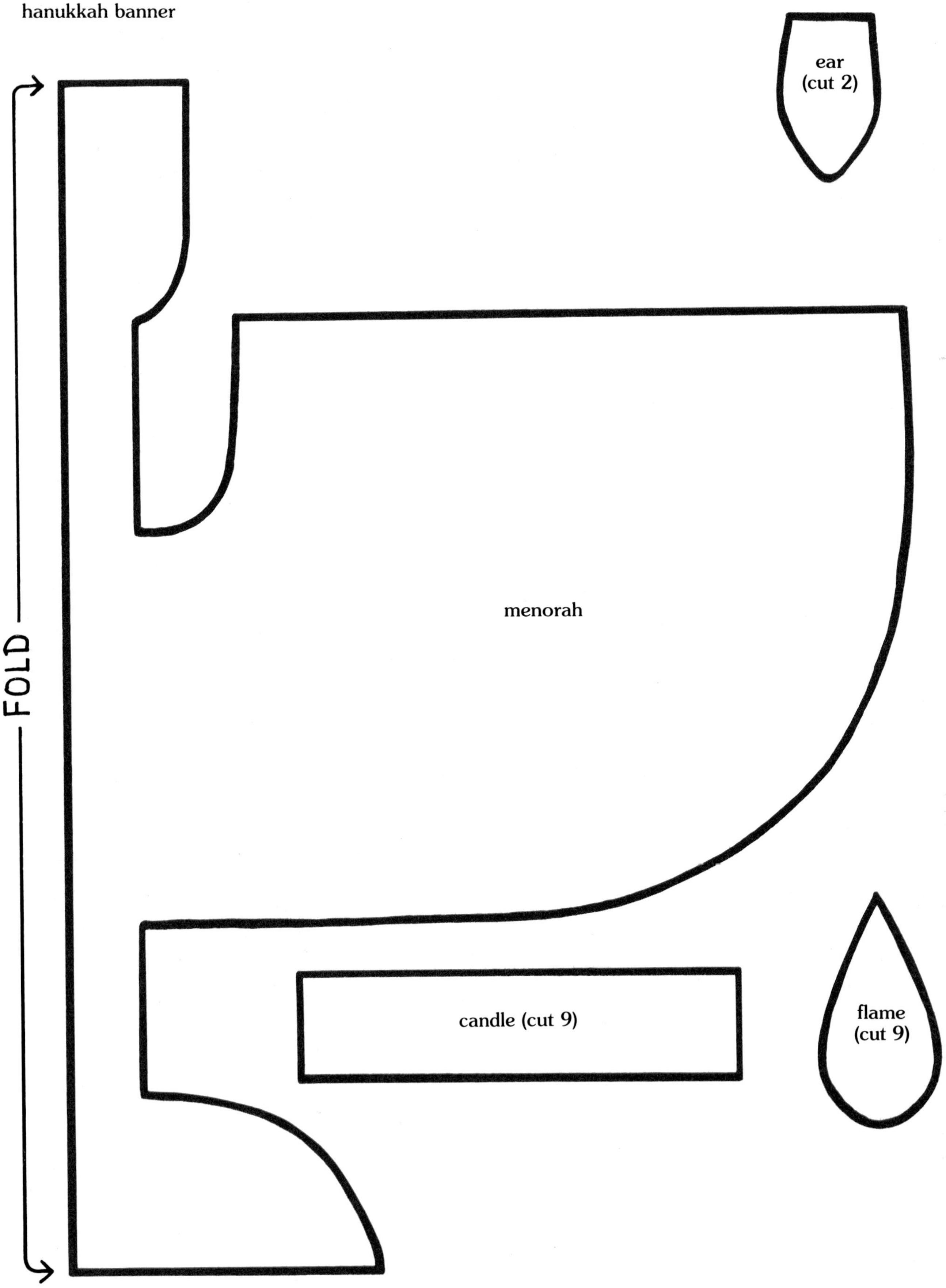

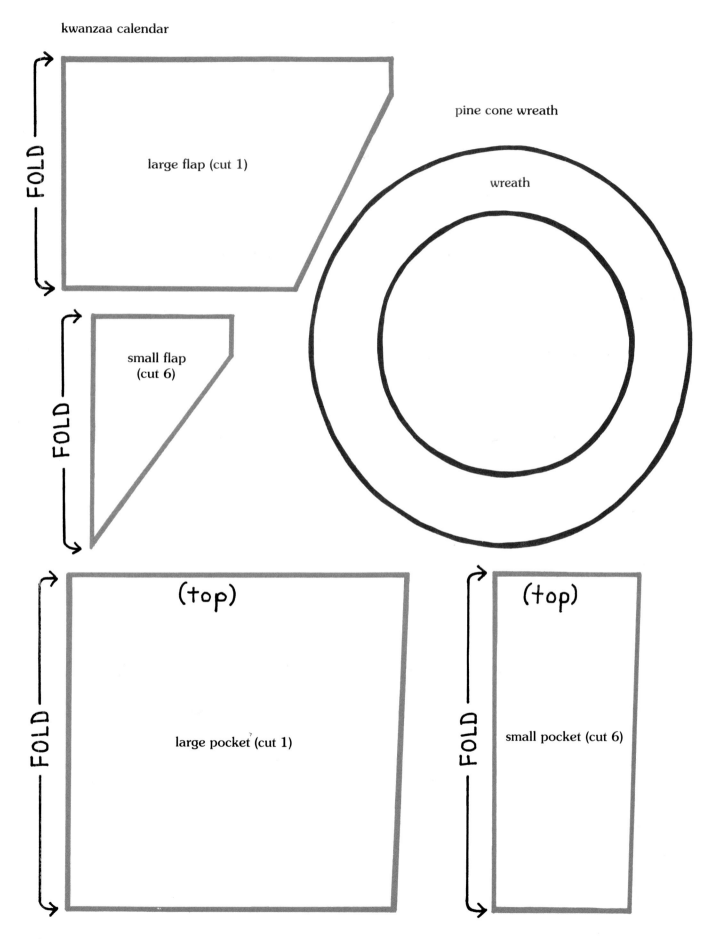

kwanzaa calendar

large flap (cut 1)

FOLD

small flap
(cut 6)

FOLD

pine cone wreath

wreath

(top)

large pocket (cut 1)

FOLD

(top)

small pocket (cut 6)

FOLD

christmas window decorations

wreath

candy cane

bell

stocking

tree